Bamburgh Castle, c. 1793

Adderstone Tower (about 4 miles south-west of Bamburgh)

Little is known about this tower. In 1415 Thomas Forster is recorded as its owner. In 1509, shortly before the battle of Flodden, Sir Thomas Forster is described as the "owner of a hold and leader of a troop of sixty horsemen".

Bamburgh Castle (on the coast, south of Holy Island)

Bamburgh is a natural and almost impregnable fortress. It was probably occupied by the Romans but comes into history as a Celtic stronghold called Dinguaroy. Legend links it with the site of King Arthur's Joyous Garde. In 547 it was seized by the English chieftain Ida, who, the *Anglo-Saxon Chronicle* informs us, "timbered Bamburgh which was at first enclosed by a hedge and afterwards by a wall". The story of Ida is probably a legend, since the quotation above was added to the Chronicle at a later date, but it was his grandson Ethelfrith who bestowed Bamburgh on his wife Bebba and from her Bamburgh derives its name (Bebban-burgh). Twice was Bamburgh besieged by the Mercian King Penda. On the first occasion he tried to set fire to the wooden walls and legend says the winds were changed by the miraculous intervention of Aidan who was then resident on Farne Island. Here was preserved the head and hand of St Oswald. Oswald being for many years the most important local saint until

1

the monks of Durham had developed the cult of St Cuthbert. An early Chronicle describes what Bamburgh was like in the 8th century:

"Bebba is a most strongly fortified city not very large, being of the size of two or three fields, having one entrance hollowed out of the rock and raised in steps after a marvellous fashion. On the top of the hill it has a church of extremely beautiful workmanship, in which is a shrine rich and costly, that contains wrapt in a pall, the right hand of St Oswald the king still incorrupt as it related by Beda the historian of this nation. To the west on the highest point of the city itself there is a spring of water, sweet to the taste and most pure to the sight, that has been excavated with astonishing labour."

With the decline of the kingdom of Northumbria the castle of Bamburgh slowly decayed, and in the 10th century was twice stormed and pillaged by the Danes. As final proof of its decline in the next century the right hand of St Oswald was stolen by a monk (the head had been purloined three hundred years earlier) and a monkish chronicler laments its ultimate disgrace. "The city," he says, "renowned formerly for the magnificent splendour of her high estate, has in these latter day been burdened with tribute and reduced to the condition of a handmaiden. She who was once the mistress of the cities of Britain has exchanged the glories of her ancient sabbaths for shame and desolation. The crowds that flocked to her festivals are now represented by a few herdsmen. The pleasures her dignity afforded us are past and gone."

Bamburgh Castle appears again on the stage of history in 1095 when Robert of Mowbray, the third Norman Earl of Northumberland revolted. William Rufus marched north and quickly overran Northumberland, shutting Mowbray up in Bamburgh. Here is the story from the *Anglo-Saxon Chronicle:*

"And then at Easter held the king his court at Winchester; and the Earl Robert of Northumberland would not come to court. And the king was much stirred to anger with him for this, and sent to him and bade him harshly, if he would be worthy of protection, that he would come to court at Pentecost. Hereafter at Pentecost was the king at Windsor, and all his council with him, except the Earl of Northumberland; for the king would neither give him hostages, nor own upon truth, that he might come and go with security. And the king therefore ordered his army and went against the Earl to Northumberland; and soon after he came thither, he won many and nearly all the best of the earl's clan in a fortress, and put them into custody; and the castle at Tinemouth he beset until he won it, and the earl's brother therein, and all that were with him; and afterwards went to Bamborough, and beset the earl therein. But when the king saw that he could not win it, then ordered he his men to make a castle before Bamborough and called it in his speech 'Malveisin'; that is in English, 'Evil Neighbour'. And he fortified it strongly with his men, and afterwards went southward. Then, soon after that the king was gone south, went the earl one night out of Bamborough towards Tinemouth; but they that were in the new castle were aware of him, and went after him, and fought him, and wounded him, and afterwards took him. And of those that were with him some they slew, and some they took alive. The king gave orders to take the Earl Robert of Northumberland, and lead him to Bamborough, and put out both his eyes, unless they that were therein would give up the castle. His wife held it, and Morel who was steward, and also his relative. Through this was the castle then given up."

Bamburgh Castle by W.Daniell, 1822

The history of Bamburgh castle during the Middle Ages is not of great interest. It was only one among many Border fortresses and by no means as important as Alnwick. It was however rebuilt and strengthened and maintained in a position of defence.

In the 17th century it came into the hands of the Forster family who squandered their estates with such reckless extravagance that they became bankrupt and their lands were put up for sale. The purchaser, in 1704, was Nathaniel Crewe, Bishop of Durham. Lord Crewe was a notorious time-serving bishop "neither a brilliant political nor ecclesiastical character, and there was nothing in his life became him like the leaving of it, since he then founded the Bamburgh Trust".

Lord Crewe died childless and the wealth he had amassed during his life was given to charities which have preserved his name. Archdeacon Sharp, the most famous of the trustees of these charities administered them well. He restored the castle, established a girls' school there, and made it a centre for succour to shipwrecked sailors. However near the end of the 19th century the *Northumberland County History* drew attention to the unsatisfactory state of the castle at that time suggesting that the school should be sited nearer the village.

Shortly afterwards the castle was purchased by the first Lord Armstrong and restored and rebuilt at considerable expense. We might only mention that the result of this restoration has been strongly criticized by many antiquarians, historians and architects. But the majestic outline of the castle as seen today is attractive from whatever angle it is viewed and we must admit the casual visitor is not particularly disturbed at the rebuilding he sees inside.

Description of castle

The entrance to Bamburgh Castle is from the south-east by a winding road leading up to a strong barbican. The outer gate is guarded by two flanking towers. Beyond is a passage cut through the rock leading to the inner bailey. On the way we pass under the Constable Tower which commands the whole entrance. The area inside covers eight acres.

In the inner bailey stands the great keep, which is earlier in date than the keep at Newcastle. The walls are massive, being over 3 m (11 feet) thick on the front, and 2.75 m (9 feet) on the other sides. The stone with which it was built was quarried at North Sunderland and they are unusually small. This was to facilitate easy portage by men or pack animals. The keep is entered by a nail studded door beneath a fine decorated Norman arch. It leads into a gloomy vaulted room on the ground floor. Hanging on the walls are two huge chains, jokingly called King Ida's watch-chains. They were formerly used for raising sunken vessels. This was done by passing them under the wrecks and buoying them at each end.

In one room of the basement is a remarkable well, 46 m (150 feet) deep half of the distance has been cut through basalt and the remainder through sandstone. It is much older than the keep, probably dating from the 8th century.

Simeon of Durham, a monk who wrote in the early 12th century in describing Bamburgh as it was in 1174 says, "There is in the western side, and in the highest part of the city, a fountain hollowed out in a marvellous fashion, and the water of which is sweet to drink and most limpid to the sight".

The wicked queen, who in the ballad of the Laidley Worm, changed her step daughter into a loathly worm is said to reside at the bottom of this well in the shape of a toad. Once every seven years she is supposed to reappear.

A mural staircase leads to the upper storeys. On the first floor is the Court Room. In this room are portraits of the two Dorothy Fosters, the first became Lady Crewe, and her niece was the heroine of Walter Besant's novel called *Dorothy Foster* which deals with the abortive revolt of 1715. Another large vaulted chamber is the armoury containing a great variety of old weapons, and another room houses the library.

Originally the Norman keep was more inhospitable than today. It was intended to serve as a final refuge in case the rest of the castle was captured or the garrison revolted. It was Dr Sharp who first made alterations so that the keep could be permanently habitable. From the top of the keep magnificent views, probably the best in Northumberland, can be seen taking in Berwick, Holy Island, the Farnes, Dunstanburgh Castle, the Cheviots and many other places.

At the south-east corner once stood the ancient Chapel of St Peter founded in the reign of Henry II. At the north end is a windmill where barley, oats and peas used to be ground for the poor of the district. On the south side are a whole range of buildings. They were erected by Lord Armstrong when he restored the castle.

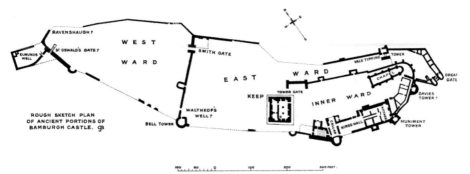

The above sketch is by Cadwallader John Bates from his History of Bamburgh Castle, 1894

Plan of Bamburgh Castle by C.J.Bates from his History of Bamburgh Castle, 1894

Bamburgh Tower (Bamburgh)

In the list of towers of 1415 there is recorded a turris de Bamburgh belonging to the master of the Austin canons. A substantial part of this tower can be seen today in the south wall of the churchyard. It is 10m (33 feet) long and the large stones project 60cm (2 feet) in front of the wall of which it now forms part.

Bathes Tower (at Spittal, just south of Berwick-upon-Tweed)

A tower belonging to the hospital of Tweedmouth once stood at Spittal. It was built by one of the masters called Bather who was appointed in 1369. In 1612 it was still known as Bathes Tower.

Craster Arms at Beadnell

Beadnell Tower (almost 2 miles south of Seahouses)

Beadnell, once an important fishing village, lies south of Seahouses. In the centre of the village stands a three-storeyed pele-tower now changed into an inn called The Craster Arms. Beadnell tower was built by the Forster family in the 16th century. On the doorsill of the inn were the initials F.I.S. 1751. The *I* and *S* probably stand for the Christian names of husband and wife and the *F* represents the name of Forster. Unfortunately this doorsill has now disappeared. By 1818 the old tower had come to serve as the back premises of a public house once called the Bull Inn.

6

A great deal of the original pele survives. The basement, now used as a beer-cellar, is vaulted and remains of the newel staircase which led to the next floor can be seen. The walls are approximately 2m (6 and 8 feet) thick. On the ground floor remains of an old fireplace are visible.

The outside of the pele was restored in the 18th century and there is now a pretty two-bayed frontage adorned with a fine coat of arms and large foliage trails carved in stone. The coat of arms belongs to the Craster family with a raven as crest and the motto *Dum vivo spero* – While there's life there's hope.

Also attached to the front is the lead sign of a Newcastle insurance company, with the insignia of three castles and the number 7058. In the days before public fire services the fire engines were controlled by insurance companies who only put out fires in buildings bearing their plaque. In the eastern wall of the inn has been inserted the carved head of a man. Its origin is uncertain.

Belford Tower (2 miles east of Budle Bay)

The tower or "fortilage" at Belford is first mentioned in 1415. It was situated at the castellated farmhouse of Belford West Hall. The remains of a moat and some foundations under green mounds could be seen in 1893. Nothing is now visible.

Berrington Tower (west of Holy Island)

In the 1541 list it is recorded as in ruins. It was in Islandshire, west of Haggerston Castle, but no trace of it can be seen today.

Berwick Castle (Berwick-upon-Tweed)

Little is left of what was once one of the most important of the Border castles. Almost all that was standing of the fortress was destroyed over a century ago to make way for the railway station. The great hall of the castle in which Edward I in 1292 declared in favour of Baliol as King of Scotland corresponds with the present station platform.

The castle has witnessed many stirring events in Border history, changing hands on more than one occasion, its history being closely linked with the fortified town of Berwick. In 1377 it was seized by seven intrepid Borderers who slew the governor, Sir Robert Boynton. They were joined by forty-one more confederates and held out for eight days against 10,000 English soldiers. Their heroism was not respected by their enemies since on surrendering the castle they were all put to the sword.

After the union of the two kingdoms the castle decayed. In 1762, "It is environed on one side by the ditch of the town; on the other by one of the same breadth, flanked by many round towers and thick walls, which enclose a large palace, in the middle of which rises a lofty keep or donjon, capable of a long resistance, and commanding all the environs of the town."

The remains of the castle which survive are the 'white wall' and a flight of steps nearby which lead down to the water tower.

Bothal Castle

Bothal Castle (west of Ashington)

Bothal, or as it used to be called Bottel, means a house or hamlet. Although it was fortified even before the Norman Conquest it wasn't until 1343 that Robert Bertram was granted permission to turn his mansion house into a castle.

The plan of the castle is that of a motte-and-bailey but the keep is the gatehouse as at Bywell and Morpeth. This gatehouse is the centre of architectural interest. The main part of the gatehouse is 12m (40 feet) by 9m

(30 feet) with two flanking semi-octagonal towers. On the battlements and the wall beneath them are carved a series of shields arranged in the following order:

THE BLACK PRINCE   EDWARD III   WAKE OF LYDEL

ACTON   GREYSTOCK   PERCY   BERTRAM   DARCY   CONYERS   FELTON

Above are two carved stone figures, representing a piper and stone-thrower. The passage through the gatehouse is 10m (33 feet) long and 3.7m (12 feet) wide and vaulted in stone. It had a portcullis, a gate, and meutrieres or openings in the roof. The masons' marks on the gate are similar to those on the barbican of Prudhoe.

The great chamber of the tower is on the first floor and possesses some interesting windows. The fine perpendicular window comes from Cockle Park from where it was removed a century ago when Bothal was being restored. The two original windows are in vaulted recesses with stone seats. The second floor is light and airy with its three Elizabethan windows. The courtyard extends for about 55m (60 yards) south of the gatehouse to the river Wansbeck. Round this courtyard, against the curtain wall, were grouped the usual domestic buildings.

In the survey of 1576 we are told Bothal was noted for its "fair gardinges and orchetts, wherein growed all kind of hearbes and floures, and fine applies, plumbes of all kynde, peers, damsellis, nuttes, wardens cherries to the black and reede, wallnutes, and also licores verie fine".

From the Bertram family Bothal descended by marriage to the Ogles and then to the Dukes of Portland.

Buckton Tower (near Holy Island)

First mentioned in the survey of 1415 it is last recorded as a farmhouse in 1581.

Burradon Tower (north-east of Newcastle)

Burradon (burg-dun meaning fort-hill) probably derives its name from an early fortification on the site. It is a colliery village about six miles from Newcastle. The tower is at Burradon farm nearby. Although its simplicity may suggest an earlier date the builder was probably Bertram Anderson of Newcastle who inherited the manor of Burradon in 1548.

9

The tower is comparatively small and is built of small rubble stones with long quoins at the angles. It stood three storeys high and the north wall is complete as far as the corbelled parapet.

The original entrance is at ground level by a low arched head doorway. Above at battlement height is a machicolation on three oversailing corbel stones, to protect the entrance. The basement is tunnel vaulted. On the first floor are the remains of a fireplace, with lintel and jambs. Earlier this century the lintel was decorated with the initials L.O. 1633 (Lancelot Ogle) but no trace remains today.

Cheswick Tower (north-west of Holy Island)

The tower of Cheswick was built after the year 1400. In 1542 it is described as "a lytle tower of the inherytaunce of one Thomas Mannors and others, being in decaye for lack of reparacions," and in 1561 it was "ruinous and in decay". The site was on the north of the village but no trace remains.

Coquet Island Tower by J.D.Harding, c. 1850

Coquet Island Tower (east of Amble)

A tower on Coquet Island, is mentioned in the list of border fortresses in 1415. The buildings on the island today belong to Trinity House and received their present form in 1840. They incorporate a large amount of original work chiefly the remains of the medieval cell of Tynemouth Priory. The lower section of the lighthouse seems to have been part of the tower of 1415. The long vaulted chamber to the north-east appears to be ecclesiastical in origin. Horsley mentions remains of a tower in 1730.

The island has been occupied intermittently during the centuries. The coal pits were once worked here along with salt pans and the stone from the quarries was considered good building material. The tower itself was undoubtedly for the defence of the monastery.

Craster Tower (on the coast, 6 miles north-east of Alnwick)

The village of Craster, formerly spelt Craucestre, probably derives its name from a camp upon Craster Heugh. Craster Tower stands half a mile inland from the village. The original tower forms part of a private residence. It is often stated that the Craster family held the estate before the Norman Conquest, but no proof exists for this claim. All we know is that Albert, the founder of the Craster family, was in possession of Craster before 1168. The tower is first mentioned in 1415 in a list of fortresses compiled in that year. It is well constructed of excellent masonry being rectangular in shape with two storeys and a vaulted basement. The battlements are modern.

The tower was added to in 1769. This Georgian wing has a fine bay front of two and a half storeys. Probably about the same time the first floor of the pele tower was converted in the Gothic taste then popular.

Craster Tower and Georgian house (after 1769)

Cresswell Tower (Druridge Bay)

The Cresswell family lived here since the days of King John, and it was probably in the 13th century that the tower was built by them. Later they erected a mansion house nearby. In the 18th century the mansion house was demolished and replaced with a new one adjoining the tower. This was destroyed less than a hundred years later when A. J. Cresswell Baker built Cresswell Hall from 1821-5. It was a building of considerable architectural interest, designed in Grecian taste by architect John Shaw. Of this hall only the extensive stables remain. But the fine old tower still stands overlooking the magnificent sands of Druridge Bay.

It consists of the byre, vaulted in stone, on the ground floor and two floors above approached by a spiral staircase. The floor of the top storey has gone. The roof turret in the north-east angle still stands and round the window was an inscription which is supposed to have read, WILLIAM CRESSWELL, BRAVE HERO.

Cresswell Tower has its ghost called the White Lady. The legend takes us back to Saxon times. The daughter of one of the barons of Cresswell had fallen in love with a Danish prince and had arranged for her lover to call and take her away. He came ashore at Druridge Bay and was approaching the tower when her three brothers waylaid and slew him before her eyes. She was stricken with grief, refused all food and drink, and starved herself to death. Her white clad ghost is supposed to be seen keeping watch on the tower roof.

Cresswell Tower and 18th century house

Detchant Tower (near Belford)

The hamlet of Detchant is two miles north-west of Belford. A tower or fortalice is mentioned here in the list of 1415, but no trace is now left.

Dunstanburgh Castle from the south-west c. 1821

Dunstanburgh Castle (on the coast, 2 miles north of Craster)

"The rugged headland on which the ruins of Dunstanburgh stand is the grandest feature in the great basalt range that traverses Northumberland and appears most prominently in the castle rock of Bamburgh, the crags of Shafto and Sewingshields, and the Nine Nicks of Thirlwall. The situation of Dunstanburgh recalls in a manner those of the other great east coast fortresses of Scarborough, Tynemouth, and Tantallon, but it is more romantic even than the last of these. No carriage road leads to Dunstanburgh, and this forced pilgrimage on foot has in itself an indescribable old-world charm. As you come along the shore from Embleton a crescent of black cliffs rises a hundred feet [30m] straight out of the waves to form the northern rampart of the castle. You almost expect to be challenged by the basalt giants that are drawn up like so many warders round the base of the stately Lilburn Tower, and might reasonably conclude that the shattered turrets of the Great Gatehouse were sustained by power of enchantment, so much do their fantastic outlines, peering mysteriously over the green slope of the western escarpment, seem to set all known principles of gravitation at defiance. High as these turrets are, in a strong north-east gale the sea dashes up through the Rumble Churn into a fountain above them. In addition to this rare combination of natural and architectural beauty, Dunstanburgh possesses historical associations of no common interest, that in their unique and melancholy character are in complete harmony with the scene." C.J.Bates.

The castle of Dunstanburgh is the largest in Northumberland and includes an area of over ten acres. It is administered by English Heritage and can be approached from Craster by a footpath along the shore. There are traces of Romano-British occupation and the ending of 'burgh' shows that it was a fortified settlement in Anglian times. In the year 1257 the barony of Embleton, which included the Manor of Dunston, passed by exchange to the popular leader Simon de Montfort. After his death at the battle of Evesham his forfeited lands were granted by Henry III to his own son Edmund, Earl of Lancaster. But the real history of Dunstanburgh Castle starts in 1313 when Thomas, Earl of Lancaster, ordered a castle to be built on the lonely rock.

"By Michaelmas 1314, sixteen perches of a moat, eighty feet [24m]broad and eighteen feet [5.5m] deep, had been dug on the west side of the castle, between it and the field of Embleton. Spanish iron had been purchased for the hinges, and the cramps for binding the stones together, and 'Eastland boards' procured for the doors and windows. Four carts and a couple of wains had been kept constantly going for stone, sand, and mortar, over and above those which the bailiff had been able to impress from the peasantry. Sea coal for burning the lime had been brought from Newcastle and elsewhere. A hostelry eighty feet

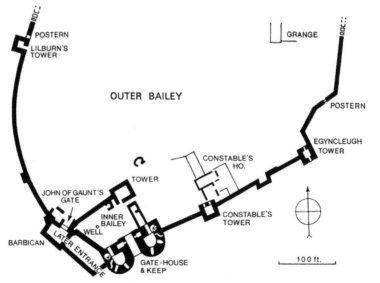

[24m] long by twenty feet [6m] broad had been erected as a shelter for the workmen at a cost of 36s. 1d., and Master Elias the mason had been proceeding with the contract he had entered into with the earl for rearing the bows of the gatehouse to the height of eighty feet[24m], with a tower above on either side of the gateway."

When the Earl was executed after his revolt and defeat at the battle of Boroughbridge in 1322 the king took over his estate and handed the custody of the castle successively to Roger Horseley, Richard of Embleton, John de Lilburn and Roger Mauduit. Dunstanburgh at this time had a small port which lay to the south of the castle. This is now marshy land cut off from the sea by a dyke.

The castle of Dunstanburgh played little part in the history of Northumberland since it was neither a border fortress nor the seat of a local lord but was controlled by the Earls of Lancaster. During the Wars of the Roses the castle changed hands twice and when the struggle was over the castle was allowed to fall into decay. In 1550 Sir Robert Bowes described it as "in wonderful great decaye". Fortunately, being remote from heavily populated areas the castle was not spoilt by modern buildings but remained a splendid ruin.

Description of castle

The main entrance to the castle is on the south and consists of two drum towers flanking an arched entrance gateway. The gatehouse forms the keep of the castle. Originally it had a barbican in front but this was removed in 1380 by John of Gaunt when he made a new entrance to the north. The great towers were three storeys high. On the second floor was the great hall, a fine room with two large mullioned windows.

Beyond the gatehouse is the inner ward which was built after the gatehouse was closed and a new gate made further north. It contains the kitchen, gatehouse and well. To the north-west corner of the inner ward are the ruins of the gate tower erected by John of Gaunt. Further along the curtain wall is the Lilburn Tower which was probably built for John Lilburn, constable of Dunstanburgh about 1325. It is well preserved and measures 9m (30 feet) square externally, with walls almost 2m (6 feet) thick. It has three storeys. The curtain wall on the north and east is of poor quality being chiefly an earth

Lilburn Tower

rampart faced with rough limestone and part has been destroyed by the sea.

The south curtain wall terminates in the Egyncleugh Tower (sometimes called Queen Margaret's Tower) which dominates the narrow inlet formerly called the Egyn Cleugh. The moat here is cut through solid rock. From Egyncleugh the curtain wall continues 55m (180 feet) to the Constable's Tower which is set astride it. Behind it are the foundations of the Constable's house. The curtain wall from the Constable's Tower to the gatehouse is thicker and of better quality than anywhere else in the castle. The moat of Dunstanburgh is a massive work being 24m (80 feet) wide and 4m (13 feet) deep. Traces of it survive. In the huge outer bailey there are traces of a number of buildings, probably cattle sheds and other farming structures.

Here's Dunstanburgh Castle's ghost story, told in the prose of Paul Brown.

"Sir Guy, valiant knight that he was, was out seeking adventure. It was the custom in his day so to do. Well mounted and well armed, he was ranging the countryside, and in the fullness of time arrived before Dunstanburgh Castle, which, I regret to say, was even then in a very poor state of repair and bore every appearance of being uninhabited. No smoke issued from chimneys, no cattle were to be seen, and every door was shut and barred. Sir Guy was annoyed about it, because dirty weather had developed and rain was coming down in torrents.

He became wetter and wetter as he rode round the outside of the castle, and, finally tying his horse to the only tree he saw—it was a yew tree—he took shelter in a porch. Somewhere he heard a bell, and at the same moment a thunderbolt whizzed past his head and burst open the door beside which he was standing.

Then it was that the bald-headed man made his appearance; and he, being an extraordinarily unpleasant person to look upon, Sir Guy ought certainly to have been upon his guard. To begin with flames were coming out of the top of his head and his whiskers were aglow with fire, and, as if these were not enough to give him away, the flowing gown he wore was covered with swastikas and abracadabras, so that there was no mistaking the fact that he was a wizard.

"Sir Knight!" said he, turning his green and glassy eyes upon Sir Guy, "if you are sufficiently brave to undertake a real man's work there is a young and beautiful lady inside this castle who is in some distress and waiting to he rescued. What about it?"

Sir Guy jumped at the offer and followed the wizard into the castle. At the top of a flight of steps they came to a great big brass door with a living bolt, a poisonous snake from whose jaws hot venom dripped and burned holes in the floor. The wizard was quite prepared, however, and presenting his red-hot iron, permitted the serpent to bite the end of it.

In a moment the gate swung open and they entered an immense hall, draped in black, and with a black-and-white marble floor. Around the apartment a hundred knights in white armour stood beside a hundred coal-black horses, and the roof was supported by a hundred columns of hammered brass, from which projected a hundred dead men's hands, holding a hundred lighted tapers which dripped blood.

Two gigantic skeletons, wearing jewelled crowns, stood at the end of the hall, the one holding a horn, once possessed by Merlin, and the other a gleaming sword, while between them was a coffin in which lay the most beautiful girl Sir Guy had ever seen.

Then up spake the wizard. He pointed to the two skeletons and said that Sir Guy's choice lay between Merlin's horn and the gleaming sword, but whichever he took hold of it was most important he should never let go until the lady was rescued.

The knight thought at once of the sword, and he was just going to seize it when somebody cried – or he thought they did – "You're wrong!" and he drew his hand away. Then grasping the horn he placed it to his lips and blew such a mighty blow that everything in the place jumped, including the hundred knights who, leaping upon their horses, charged at him as one man.

Throwing aside the horn he drew his own sword and was prepared to fight. The inevitable happened. Sir Guy suddenly found himself outside the castle beside the yew tree and with the rain pouring down upon him.

For many years he has been trying to find his way again to make an appointment with the lovely lady. He is old now, a ghost without a shadow, and his white locks and overgrown beard flutter in the salt breezes. His cries of anguish are frequently heard at midnight."

Dunstanburgh Castle: window in north-east tower   *window in the gateway*   *C.Jewitt*

Dunston Tower
See Proctor Steads

Elwick Towers (on Fenham Flats, to the south of Holy Island)
In the list of towers, compiled in 1415, two towers are mentioned in Elwick, that of Thomas de Bradforth and that of Thomas de Elwick. The same two towers are mentioned in 1561.

Embleton Tower (about 6 miles north-east of Alnwick)
This is a typical Northumbrian vicar's pele. It was built in 1395 at a cost of £40 as a consequence of a recent Scottish raid in which a band "lay in the fields of Emelden and did great destruction". It is mentioned as the vicar's property in 1415. In 1828 large additions were made to the house by Dobson, the famous Newcastle architect.

The tower is remarkable for having two vaulted chambers in the basement divided by a central wall. The entrance from the modern wing was probably at first floor level.

*Farne Island
Tower c. 1790*

Farne Island Tower
(offshore from Bamburgh)

Speede's 1611 map

The tower was built by Thomas Castell, Prior of Durham from 1494 to 1519. It is a typical Border pele, originally of four stories. It has a vaulted basement and stone staircase, partly spiral. The so-called well of St Cuthbert is on the ground floor, the normal place in a pele tower. It originally stood at the rear of a courtyard with a fortified gate flanked by two chapels. Above the gate was a turret. These details can be seen on Speed's map of 1611. Prior Castell's tower for a long time served as the first lighthouse upon Farne. The beacon was a fire of coals, which was nightly kindled upon its summit by a person who lived in the adjoining ruined church.

Fenham Castle (near Holy Island)
Remains of a motte-and-bailey castle can be traced on the south side of the road which goes from the village of Fenham to the mill. We know nothing of its history and it seems an unusual place for such an early fortification to be placed.

Fenham Tower (near Holy Island)
The manor house of the monks of Holy Island was in existence in 1339. It lay just across the water from their priory on the island. Their servant there was paid £5 13s. 4d. in 1339 and "48 acres were sown with wheat, 19 with barley, and 50 with pease and oats". The building was described in 1560 as a "tower in good reparacions" and in the following year was leased to the Crown under the name of 'The Grange'. At the end of the 18th century large parts of the building were still standing. James Raine says he was able to trace in 1826 the foundations of many rooms showing the house was of considerable size. There were also signs of the moat which the monks had dug for their defence. In a field to the west called Ducket Close Canon Raine traced the foundations of a dovecote.

In 1603 Sir William Reade now old and blind was living at the tower. We are told that James VI of Scotland on his way south to take the throne of England visited him on his journey from Berwick to Widdrington. "The way his majesty had to ride being long, enforced him to stay with this good Knight the lesse while; but that time was so comfortable that his friends hope it will be a meane to cherish the old Knight all his life long". Sir William died a few months later.

Goswick Pele (near Holy Island)
Goswick pele was not mentioned in the early Border surveys but in 1560 there was a "pile" here which helps to date the building closely. It was for many centuries the home of the Swinhoes. When Raine published his *History of North Durham* in 1852 the house had been altered so much that its character could not be ascertained. It had been converted into farm buildings and other "vile uses". It stood on the sea front, near the mouth of the brook looking towards Holy Island, but nothing is now left.

Haggerston Castle (near Holy Island)
In 1311 Edward II received the homage of Thomas, Earl of Lancaster, in the manor-house of the Haggerstons. Licence to crenellate was given in 1345. In 1541 it was described "as a strong tower in a good state of repair". In 1618 it was almost destroyed by fire but a large square tower was left standing and this was incorporated in a mansion built some time before 1777. In 1805 more rebuilding took place, likewise in 1889. All that now remains is a tall tower with yet a higher stair-turret. Because of the rebuilding at various times we cannot give a date to the present remains.

Holy Island Castle (about 10 miles south of Berwick-upon-Tweed, offshore)
The Castle on Holy Island owes its existence to an Order in Council issued in 1539 ordaining that "all havens should be fensed with bulwarks and bloke houses against the Scots". In 1543, on the occasion of Lord Hertford's raid into Scotland 2,220 soldiers were landed on the island and ten line-of-battle ships anchored in the harbour. In 1548-9 King Edward VI's engineers were ordered "to view the place by the church what hill or grounds were mete for fortification there". Building started immediately using stone from the ruined priory and in the Border Survey of 1550 it is first mentioned as the "Fort of Beblowe which Iyeth very well for the defense of the haven". The garrison was not large. In 1559 it consisted of a non-resident captain, two master gunners at 1s. per day, a master's mate at 10d. per day, and twenty soldiers at 8d. per day. A report to the Crown made in 1561 has some interesting information.

Holy Island Castle by Ronald Embleton

"The Holy Iland is scituate within the sea, and yit at every tyde of lowe water
men may passe into the same on horseback or foote, and it is in compasse about
iijor myles by estimat or more, and hath in the same a little borowgh towne, all
sett with fishers very poore, and is a markett town on ye Satterday, howbeit it is
little vsed, and yit by reason thereof all the townes of Norham and Ilandshyre
ought theire to receive yr measors and wights, and are in all things to be
directed by thassisse of the said towne of Iland. And there was in the same Iland
one Cell of Monks of the house of Durham, which house hath the personage of
the said parish as before is declared, which mansione howse was build in fovre
square of two Courts, as appeareth by the platt theirof, and nowe the same
howse in the Quene's Maties storehouse and also another howse in the towne
called the Pallace, which is the newe brewehouse and bakehouse, and other
offices in the same for the said storehouse. And in the same Iland is also one
forte builded vpon an hill called Beblowe, which serveth very well for the
defence and saveguard of the heaven, the which haven is a very good and apt
haven both of the harborowe and landinge. The inhabitants there have baylifs
and all other officers of their owne elections yerely, charged at Michmas, and
have certeine men which be burgesses and fremen, of wch companie the sayd
officers be always chosen. And everye burgesse payeth certen burrowe rent, save

21

Dining Room

xij or xiij, which clame to be free that they never payd anye burrowe fearme. The moreparte of the towne is nowe decayed in howses, and yit the tofts and crofts where howses did stand remayne, of which the burrowe rent in nowe for the most part collected and raysed, as hereafter doth appeare."

Although the castle lost its importance with the union of England and Scotland under James I it still remained a government fortress. John Aston who visited it in 1639 described it as a "pretty fort recently repaired and put into forme". There were two batteries and "on the lower stood mounted three iron peeces and two of brasse, with carriadges and platformes in good order. On the higher was one brasse gunne and two iron ones with all ammunition to them. There are twenty four men and a captain kept in pay to man it, the common souldiours have 6d. per diem". The governor was Captain Rugg, described by another visitor as "famous for his generous and free entertainment of strangers, as for his great bottle nose, which is the largest I have seen".

During the Civil War the castle came into the hands of the Parliamentary forces but its importance as a military base was over. Slowly it fell into decay although a garrison was maintained until 1820. It was then converted into a coastguard station and later became the headquarters of an Island detachment of the Northumberland Artillery Volunteers.

In 1903, Edward Hudson of *Country Life*, on a visit to the island found the castle a ruin. With the aid of Sir Edwin Lutyens the famous architect he had the castle restored as a home to live in.

Description of castle

The castle now consists of two batteries, the lower facing south-east and the upper due south. The buildings form two blocks at right angles. The entry hall is completely modern and leads to two plain vaulted chambers known as the Dining Room and Ship Room. They were originally magazines and the original stonework and brick floors have not been greatly altered. On the second floor are bedrooms facing south and east. They are joined by a long gallery which reminds one of a ship's deck.

The rooms are filled with a fine collection of antique furniture, mostly oak, of English or Flemish of the early 17th century. Ornaments and pictures are all in harmony making a unique and picturesque home. The castle and its contents were given to the National Trust in 1944.

Hoppen Tower (3 miles south-west of Bamburgh)

Hoppen lies three miles from Bamburgh and is now only a farmstead. The family first appear on the list of jurors who assessed the subsidy to be paid by Bamburgh ward in 1296. The tower here first appears in the list of 1415 and belonged to Robert Hoppen. It is never mentioned again and no trace remains.

Horton Castle (near Blyth)

Horton is situated four miles south-west of Blyth on a high ridge. Here there stood till 1809, on the site of Low Horton Farm, a strong castle defended by a double moat and rampart of earth. It is unfortunate that the castle was destroyed, since it was an example of the true type of pele or fortified enclosure.

Guiscard de Charron obtained permission in 1292 to fortify his manor house here and completed the work in six years. The castle was later held by the Monbouchers and finally the Delavals who left it in the 17th century.

Howick Tower (5 miles north-east of Alnwick)

The medieval tower of Howick was destroyed in 1780, when Howick Hall was built from designs by Newton of Newcastle. It is first mentioned in 1415 when Emeric Hering was its owner. In 1538 it is described as a "little pile, a mile from the shore". The present hall was built in 1782, with alterations made in 1809. It was rebuilt after a fire in 1926.

The view of Howick Hall was drawn by Thomas Allom in 1832. The owner Earl Grey had that year been the architect of the famous Reform Bill. "The west front of this elegant mansion," we are told, "is seen to great advantage in this view and forms, with the wings and connecting buildings, an imposing and splendid coup d'oeil. The lawn sweeps in a magnificent slope to the margin of a fine trout water which, after flowing through the shrubberies and plantations, passes away by a gentle fall. The gardens are perfect 'realms of fairy', enriched with every species of native flowers and exotics, on which flora has bestowed a more than ordinary richness of scent or beauty of appearance."

Howick Hall by Thomas Allom, 1832

Kyloe Tower (south-west of Holy Island at East Kyloe)
It is first mentioned as belonging to David Grey who died in 1450. It was inhabited till 1633. The present remains are attached to farm buildings. The original (now blocked) doorway and the complete tunnel vaulted ground floor are all that remain. The walls are 2.5m (8 feet) thick but the tower was not high or extensive.

Little Houghton Tower (about 3 miles north-east of Alnwick)
Little Houghton Tower, for many years the home of the Roddam family, lies two miles east of Howick Hall. Here the remains of the medieval tower have a wing on one side dated 1686 and on the other a Georgian building. The tower was only mentioned once (probably because of its small size) as late as 1734, being described as a building "remarkable as a strong tower of great antiquity". The tower was partially demolished in 1818 but a visitor who saw it before then recorded that it was 7.6m (25 feet) square with walls 1.5m (5 feet) thick, a vaulted basement and a corner newel staircase. The large door was square-headed.

Lowick Tower (about 8 miles south of Berwick)

The village of Lowick lies 4 miles west of Holy Island. In 1388 a "forclet" is mentioned here as belonging to Sir Alan Heton. The tower is mentioned in 1415, 1514, 1541 and 1580. In 1584 a report said £50 was needed for repair but nothing seems to have been done. The north corner of Lowick Hall Farm once called Bastle Corner, may be the site.

Newlands Tower (near Belford)

In 1310 John de Middleton was granted licence to crenellate "mansum suum de Neulond". Newland tower, near Belford is mentioned in the 1415 list but nothing is known of its history, size or exact location.

Newstead Tower (5 miles south-west of Bamburgh)

The tower at Newstead, along with Alnham, was held by the Earl of Northumberland's adherents in 1405. The list of 1415 mentions it as belonging to Sir Robert Ogle. A few years later it came into the hands of the Percys. Writing to Henry VIII in 1532 the Earl of Northumberland reported that the Scots had "brunte a towne of myne called Alenam . . . and tooke up annother towne of myne called Newstede, 200 hed of cataill, 26 presoners, and haithe shamefully murdered 2 yonge spryngaldes, the eldest of theyme not above 15 yere olde". The last we hear of the tower is in 1536 during the 'Pilgrimage of Grace'.

Newtown Pele (north-west of Bamburgh)

The present farm of Newtown at the mouth of the Waren burn near Bamburgh is probably on the site of the ancient Warenmouth. The tower here is first mentioned in an old conveyance of 1628. In 1715 we read, "Newtown: a small village where are ye remains of an ancient pile; Ralph Brandling, esq". On a map of 1781 when Newtown belonged to the Greys, a bastle is marked.

North Sunderland Tower (west of Seahouses)

There are no written records of this tower which was demolished about 1790 to provide a site for the church. The *Northumberland County History* describes the remains before demolition: "It was square, and of solid masonry; the walls being about five feet [1.5m] in thickness. It consisted of two storeys, the lower of which was perfect, having an arched roof of stone, with a large doorway to the north, and communicating with the upper storey by a hanging stair in the south-west angle of the building. Of this upper storey portions of the walls were standing, but it was roofless, with an accumulation of debris on the floor which was overgrown with grass and weeds. The tower appears to have been about 24 feet [7.3m] square. A hammered cannon ball was found by the sexton when digging a grave within twenty yards [18m] of the site of the tower. Whilst the tower was in course of demolition several score of coins from the reign of Elizabeth to that of Anne were discovered. No trace of this ancient building now remains."

Outchester Tower (south-west of Bamburgh)
Outchester, near Bamburgh, derives its name from the camp which can still be traced. In the 15th century it was a large village with two rows of houses and in a deed of 1462 a tower is mentioned as attached to the residence of the owner of the manor. It is last recorded in 1547 when Nicholas Horsley bequeathed his manor tower and other houses and lands in Outchester to his son John.

Preston Tower (7 miles north of Alnwick)
The modern mansion of Preston Tower stands about a mile to the south-east of Ellingham. The house was built on the site of old Preston Hall which was destroyed by fire in 1782. In the grounds are the remains of Preston Tower which is first mentioned in the List of Fortalices of 1415. It was originally a long

building with towers at the four corners. Two of these towers and the connecting wall remain today.

The building is now used as a clock tower, the clock occupying one of the windows in the second floor. Its bell was cast in Newcastle. The restoration was carried out in 1864 by Henry Baker Cresswell. At the time several cottages which adjoined the tower were removed. Traces of them can still be seen in the stonework.

Proctor Steads

Proctor Steads (near Craster)

The hamlet of Dunston adjoins the grounds of Craster Tower. Nearby is a group of buildings called Dunston Hall or Proctor Steads. The oldest part is a pele tower which is supposed to have been an outpost of Dunstanburgh Castle. It consists of four stages. The basement, which is vaulted as usual, is built entirely of basalt. It is of very early date, some claiming it be of Saxon workmanship. The superstructure of freestone was probably built at the same time as Dunstanburgh Castle. Adjoining the pele is an interesting 17th century hall. On the lintel of the doorway are the letters J.P. and the date 1652. The property came into the hands of John Proctor in 1705 and the name was changed.

Rock Hall Tower (4 miles north-east of Alnwick)

Four miles to the north-east of Alnwick is the charming village of Rock which lies just outside the gate of Rock Hall, a picturesque building with its ivy covered walls, mullioned windows and battlemented roof. It has been built at different times. The central part of the house is an oblong tower which dates from the late 15th century. Two smaller towers of a later date are attached to it. A large manor house was added in the 17th century by the Salkelds. Their arms appear above three sundials, two of which bear the date 1670. Colonel John

Salkeld (1616-1705) was a prominent Royalist. At the age of twenty-seven he murdered John Swinburne of Capheaton near the gates of Meldon but managed to escape punishment. He served Charles I "with a constant, dangerous and expensive loyalty as volunteer captain, and colonel of horse," as his epitaph claims.

The hall was burnt down in 1752 but was restored in 1809 by Charles Bosanquet, the architect being John Dobson. This print of the hall was published in 1826, but shows the hall before restoration.

Scremerston Tower (2 miles south of Berwick-upon-Tweed)

The tower or fortalice of Scremerston is first mentioned in 1402. In 1542 it is described as "a great old towre, much decayed for lacke of contynuall necessary reparacons". In 1560 it is called a "good towre, with a barmekin in good reparacions". After the accession of James VI to the throne of England it fell into disrepair. It stood in a field north of the village.

Seaton Delaval Tower (9 miles north-east of Newcastle)

It is first mentioned in 1415, but no licence to crenellate exists so we cannot establish its date. The site is not known but is thought to have stood close to the present hall. In 1549 the beacon on the tower head formed one of a chain of fires prepared to warn of invasion. In 1628 it was considerably enlarged by Sir Robert Delaval. But it was sadly decayed when Admiral Delaval came to live here in 1718 and two years later Vanbrugh demolished it to make way for the magnificent hall he erected on the site.

Seghill Tower (7 miles north-east of Newcastle)

This tower is first mentioned in the list of fortalices of 1415. Only the vaulted basement remains and was used as a beer and coal cellar by the old Blake Arms Hotel. It is tunnel vaulted with transverse unchamfered ribs.

There are at least eleven bays indicating that the tower was one of the largest in the county. It is said to have been of three storeys with a lofty turret at one corner. It was considerably altered in 1673.

The vault of Seghill Tower, 1834

Shilbottle Tower (3 miles south of Alnwick)

The pele tower is mentioned in a list of Northumbrian fortalices in 1415 as the "tower of Schilbotyl". It was not originally a vicarage pele but in 1526 it was occupied by Charles Watson who paid a rent of 12d a year for it. The adjoining house is a modern addition and the third floor of the tower was added in 1863.

The upper storey (now the second floor) is lighted by two trefoil-headed windows and the first floor by two lancets. On the side next to the churchyard is inserted a panel inscribed with a verse which may have been taken from an old tombstone to be seen at Melrose Abbey.

> The earth goeth on the earth
> Glistring like gold,
> The earth goes to the earth
> Sooner than it wold.
> The earth builds on the earth
> Castles and towers,
> The earth says to the earth
> All shall be ours.

Togston Tower (2 miles south-west of Amble)
Although not mentioned in the list of fortalices of 1415 a tower stood here until 1820 when it was taken down by its owner "to his subsequent, and lasting regret".

Tweedmouth Tower (on opposite bank of Tweed from Berwick)

Tweedmouth is on the south side of the Tweed opposite Berwick. Founded at an early period it was long used by the English kings as a base of operations against Berwick. Tweedmouth was a portion of the patrimony of St Cuthbert and continued to belong to the Bishops of Durham until Elizabethan times.

There are notices at different times of a small castle at Tweedmouth probably built by an early Bishop of Durham in connection with the bridge. In 1202 King John wishing to get control of Berwick, then part of Scotland, strengthened this fortress but William the Lion twice destroyed it. During the following centuries it is occasionally mentioned the last time being in 1753. Its site is unknown.

Tynemouth Castle and Priory

Tynemouth Castle (on the coast, east of Newcastle)

The history of Tynemouth Castle is closely connected with that of the Priory, both of which stand on the same rocky headland. Setting aside the idea of a Roman occupation there is the tradition that it was used as a military base by the Danish invaders. We are on certain ground in 1095 when William Rufus captured "Earl Robert's castle which is at the mouth of the river Tyne". Earl Robert de Mowbray's castle from which he defied the king was probably of earthern ramparts surmounted by a wooden stockade.

In 1296 Edward granted the prior and convent of Tynemouth permission to surround their monastery with a wall of stone. The medieval walls and tower, with the exception of the gatehouse, which survive, belong to that period.

In 1390 the gatehouse was erected on the landward side. It is a powerful gatehouse keep with a barbican in front. In 1538 the convent was disbanded and the lands attached to it were taken over by the king who granted them to Sir Thomas Hilton of Hilton. The castle, however remained in royal hands and in 1545 a thousand workmen were employed in fortifying the headland. When the work was completed a garrison of Spanish mercenaries was stationed here (hence the name of the Spanish Battery). During the Civil War the castle played an important part but afterwards fell into decay. In 1681 it was in a ruinous state and the defence of the Tyne was taken over by the newly built Clifford's Fort at North Shields.

At the beginning of the 20th century the castle was a barracks with many buildings added to it. But in 1936 after being gutted by fire it was taken over by a forerunner of English Heritage. Many additions have been removed and the original parts of the castle have been restored to a more dignified form.

Description of castle

As at Dunstanburgh, Bywell and Bothal the strength of Tynemouth castle lay in its gatehouse. It consists of an oblong tower with a projecting barbican like Alnwick and Prudhoe. The entrance through the barbican was by a vaulted passage protected by a portcullis and gate flanked by towers whose basements were used as guard rooms. The open court further on was originally a drawbridge pit separating the barbican from the gatehouse. A second vaulted passage with guard rooms at the side passes under the gatehouse.

On the first floor of the gatehouse is the magnificent great hall with a wide fireplace, lighted on all sides by windows since modernized. Adjoining is the kitchen with its wide fireplace and huge oven. Above the great hall is the great chamber.

Formerly the entire promontory was enclosed by a curtain wall and towers. The west wall in now nearly all Elizabethan but a fragment of the medieval Whitley Tower still survives. To the south of the gatehouse were two towers which are now mere earthworks revetted in stone for artillery. Most of the south wall was destroyed in 1851 but a medieval tower still stands. The north and east walls have fallen into the sea.

Warkworth Castle (6 miles south-east of Alnwick)

The castle of Warkworth stands on a lofty eminence on the south side of the Coquet overlooking the village. The hill rises precipitously from the river on the west with a more gradual slope on the east. The only level approach is from the south which is heavily guarded with a moat and flanking towers and the great gate of the castle.

"Warkworth," writes Mr Freeman, "of less historical fame than Alnwick, is in itself a more pleasing object of study. It stands as a castle should stand, free from the disfigurement of modern habitation." It is only by chance that Warkworth was not ruined by restoration, for when the estate came into the hands of the Duke of Somerset by his marriage to the heiress of the last Earl of Northumberland he considered restoring Warkworth instead of Alnwick.

Warkworth. Old print by T.Girtin, 1797

The name of Warkworth in the 12th century was Werceworde, that is the home of a woman called Werce. But it first comes into the light of history when in 737 Ceolwulf, king of Northumbria, bestowed it on the monks of Lindisfarne. The first fortifications, apart from what remained of the Saxon stronghold, were erected about 1140 by Henry, son of David I of Scotland. In 1158 Henry II granted the "castle and manor" to Roger Fitz Richard whose descendents held it for almost two hundred years when it passed into the hands of the Percys. When William the Lion came to Warkworth in 1173 he "did not deigne to stop there, for weak was the castle, the wall and the trench".

The Percys took over in 1332. The most famous of the family who were connected with Warkworth were the first Earl of Northumberland and his son Harry Hotspur whose name is enshrined in ballad as the hero of the battles of Otterburn and Homildon Hill. They were chiefly responsible for placing Henry IV on the throne in 1399 but later conspired against him. Hotspur was killed at the battle of Shrewsbury and Henry marched north to batter the castle of Warkworth into submission. Three of the scenes in Shakespeare's *Henry the Fourth, Part 1*, are laid at Warkworth. He describes it as "this worm-eaten hold of ragged stone, where Hotspur's father, old Northumberland, lies crafty-sick". Many years later, in 1569, the Percys took part in the Rising of the North and their estates were forfeited when the rebellion failed.

The castle was plundered by Sir John Forster, the Warden of the Middle Marches, who did damage that was "gret and marvellous". So much so that when James I came to Warkworth in 1617 he looked at the Percy Lion on the keep and asserted "this Iyone houldes up this castle". His retinue were "much moved to see it soe spoyled and so badly kept". More damage was done in 1672 when John Clarke, the estate auditor, took away 272 wagon loads of lead, timber, and other materials to build his house at Chirton. In 1922 the castle was placed under the care of a forerunner of English Heritage.

Gatehouse. Drawn and engraved by James Kerr.

Description of castle

The castle follows closely the plan of a motte-and-bailey with which it began its history. The keep stands upon an artificial mound and is about one hundred paces from the gatehouse which was the main entrance.

The gatehouse is a fine example of early English work. In front is a ditch which originally would be crossed by a drawbridge, the recess for which can still be seen. The large corbels higher up support machicolations through which the defenders could pour down arrows, lead or boiling water on the attackers below. Near them are square holes, which can be found right round the castle walls. They carried the timber supports for a wooden gallery with openings and arrow slits in its floor. Behind the drawbridge was a door, then a portcullis and an inner iron gate. The passage between was very dangerous since it was exposed to fire from the guardrooms with their arrow slits on either side.

Within the gate lies the bailey or courtyard. On three sides are the ruins of buildings clinging to the curtain wall. To the left within the gatehouse are the ruins of a chapel. Next comes the solar or private chamber which rises above the cellar. They stand behind the Carrickfergus Tower which was defended by crossbowmen. We next come to the great hall which was entered by the Lion Tower and adjoining are the buttery and kitchen. The Lion Tower derives its name from the carved figure of a "portentous lion, of a race certainly now extinct, with a vast frill round his neck by way of mane, the quaint ugliness of his features being mellowed by the touch of time". It was built in the second half of the 15th century.

Close to the tower is a large blue stone of which the following tale is told. One night the custodian of the castle dreamed three times that there lay beneath a blue stone, a buried treasure. He told his dream to a neighbour but allowed three days to elapse before looking for the blue stone. He soon found a trench, newly dug, and on the edge a blue stone which he had not seen before. His neighbour shortly afterwards grew mysteriously rich.

On the eastern wall is the Grey Mare's Tail tower. It has been described as the most remarkably perfect specimen of early 13th century military architecture with the finest examples in Europe of loopholes designed for crossbow shooting.

The best preserved part of the castle is the keep. It is "a good study of the process by which the purely military castle gradually passed into the house fortified for any occasional emergency". It was considerably altered in the 16th century and later restored and refaced in 1853-8 by Anthony Salvin. The outstanding feature is the central 'lantern' which gives light internally to most of the rooms and provided rain water for very advanced sanitary arrangements.

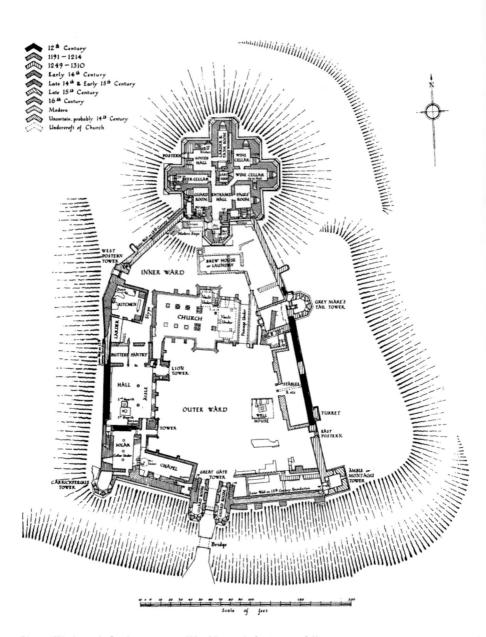

Legend:

- 12th Century
- 1191 – 1214
- 1249 – 1310
- Early 14th Century
- Late 14th & Early 15th Century
- Late 15th Century
- 16th Century
- Modern
- Uncertain, probably 14th Century
- Undercroft of Church

POSTERN
GOODS HALL
LARDER & TANK ROOM
WINE CELLAR
BEER CELLAR
WINE CELLAR
GUARD ROOM
ENTRANCE HALL
PAGES' ROOM

Modern Steps

WEST POSTERN TOWER

BREW HOUSE or LAUNDRY

INNER WARD

KITCHEN

LARDER

BUTTERY PANTRY

CHURCH
Vaults Under
Passage Under

GREY MARE'S TAIL TOWER

LION TOWER

HALL

AISLE

STABLES

OUTER WARD

WELL HOUSE

TURRET

EAST POSTERN

TOWER

SOLAR

Cellar Under

CHAPEL

GREAT GATE TOWER

AMBLE or MONTAGU TOWER

CARRICKFERGUS TOWER

GUARD ROOM
GUARD ROOM

Outer Wall on 13th Century Foundations

Bridge

Scale of feet

Plan of Warkworth Castle courtesy of Her Majesty's Stationery Office

The ground floor which is entirely vaulted is entered by a modern doorway. In the vestibule there is a hidden pit below the floor. Beyond is the entrance hall from which lead off storerooms, guard room, wine cellar and pages' room. The staircase leads up to the ante-room of the great hall on the first floor. On the western side are the buttery, pantry and great kitchen with huge fireplaces. Adjoining is the chapel which is lighted by three tall traceried windows through which a fine view of the sea can be obtained.

Warkworth (The Bridge Tower)

The bridge at Warkworth was built in the last quarter of the 14th century. The bridge has two ribbed arches and sharp triangular cutwaters. England has very few fortified bridges and the Bridge Tower at Warkworth is unique for this county. It is a small and simple gateway of two storeys. Unfortunately the parapet and machicolations have disappeared.

OLD TOWER AND BRIDGE AT WARKWORTH

Tower and bridge at Warkworth

Whitley Tower (9 miles north-east of Newcastle)

In 1345 Gilbert de Whitley was granted a licence to crenellate his manor house at Whitley [Whitley Bay]. There are no remains of this tower left and the site is not now known. It is mentioned in the survey of 1415 but at no later date.

East view of Widdrington Castle by S.& N.Buck, 1728

Widdrington Castle (just over a mile inland from Druridge Bay)

Of the old castle, crenellated by Gerard de Widdrington in 1341, nothing remains. It was pulled down about 1767 and it is said the stones were used to build workmen's homes. The site is now marked by a low green mound approached by a row of lime trees locally called the 'Twelve Apostles'.

James I stayed here on his journey to London to be crowned. His visit was described as follows:

"Long as the miles were, his majestie made short worke, and attained Witherington, where, by the master of the place, Sir Robert Carey and his right vertuous lady, he was received with all duty and affection: the house being plentifully furnished for his entertainment. Besides for scituation and pleasure it standes very delightful. His majestie having a little while reposed himselfe after his great journey, found new occasion to travel further; for as he was delighting himselfe with the pleasure of the parke, he suddenly beheld a number of deere neare the place. The game being so faire before him he could not forbear, but according to his wonted manor forth he went and slew two of them, which done, he returned with a good appetite to the house where he was most royally feasted and banketted that night."

We are told that Sir George Warren who pulled down the old building intended to erect a new mansion on the site. He asked a friend to suggest a design for the building and he was given a view of the castle he had destroyed made in 1728 by the brothers S. and N. Buck. The new mansion house was nearly complete when it was gutted by fire. Once more the work started and a new building arose described as "a slight fantastical, insulated building possessing neither grandeur nor convenience". This was demolished in 1862.

The Widdringtons are only remembered today for the legendary exploit of Richard Widdrington at the Battle of Chevy Chase.

> For Witherington my heart was woe,
>> that ever he slain should be;
> For when both his legs were hewn in two
>> yet he kneeled and fought on his knee.

Or as another version has it:

> For Witherington needs must I wayle
>> as one in dolefull dumps,
> For when his legs were smitten off
>> he fought upon his stumps.

The Widdringtons were staunch Jacobites and the fourth Lord William, with his two brothers joined the rising of 1715. They were captured at Preston and tried for treason. Although their lives were spared their estates were confiscated and the family disappeared.

Widdrington Castle as built in 1772

Glossary of terms

Bailey see **motte-and-bailey**. Later, the open area enclosed by the castle walls. Same as **ward**. There were several buildings in the bailey which served as the domestic quarters, the keep being intended primarily for defence, not residence.

Barbican see **gatehouse**

Barmkin (also barmekyn) bailey of a pele or bastle.

Basement lowest floor of a tower (not necessarily below ground level), usually stone vaulted – simply barrel-arched in the case of the peles and bastles. **Vaulted** – arched, stone roofed room intended to be fire resistent.

Bastle (bastel) smaller version of a pele. A stone built two storey house with walls some 1.5 metres (5 feet) thick. Vaulted ground floor for livestock. External access to first floor living accommodation by steps or ladder.

Battery fortified emplacement for heavy guns. **Magazine** – store for arms and ammunition.

Battlements parapet with gaps (**crenels/ embrasures**) between the upstanding **merlons**. Same as **crenellations**. **Castellated** – having battlements.

Chamfer to smooth out the pronounced angle between two surfaces by making a third surface.

A 16th century two-storey bastle house showing the usual narrow door at one end of the lower storey and the door above the steps to the upper room.

Corbel projecting support in wood or stone to support a larger projecting structure above

Curtain wall inner wall and joining towers around a castle. The term **shell-keep** describes a curtain wall with residential buildings constructed against its inner side, Alnwick Castle is a good example.

Donjon early term for a keep.

Gatehouse building guarding the main entrance to a castle. This stone structure could include a **drawbridge** (a bridge lowered from the gatehouse over a moat), a **portcullis** (a wood and metal grating dropped vertically from above), **machicolations** (crenellated parapet above with openings for pouring liquid and dropping missiles on the heads of the enemy) and loopholes for firing arrows. In turn the gatehouse sometimes had its own defensive building in front – the **barbican**.

Keep main tower of a castle. The keep of the castle in Newcastle was massively built with walls almost 5.5 metres (some 18 feet) thick at the base.

Licence to crenellate permission from the king to fortify an existing house; the first licences being granted to owners of manor-houses in 1195. The usual method was to dig a moat, construct a tower and erect a palisade.

Lintel and Jamb top (lintel) and side (jamb) supports of a fireplace, window or door.

List of Fortalices 1415 (also 1541) survey into the condition of Border towers and castles.

Meurtrieres 'murder holes' in the roofs of passageways for dropping missiles on attackers below.

Motte-and-bailey **motte** or artificial earth mound for keeps of the 11th and 12th centuries. Usually with a wood or stone tower on the mound surrounded by a **palisade** (timber fence) and then a ditch. The **bailey** being the open area enclosed by the fence. These early fortresses were often rebuilt in stone – the keep first, then the walls – to form the Norman castles we see today. Unlike the Anglo-Saxons who built defensive *burghs* – to defend the community against invaders – the invading Normans (1066) embarked on a rapid